Written in Sand

Also by Antony Fawcus and published by Ginninderra Press
Storms (Pocket Poets)
The Ethiopian Afar

Antony Fawcus

Written in Sand

Written in Sand
ISBN 978 1 76041 102 7
Copyright © Antony Fawcus 2016
Cover image: Anna Fawcus

First published 2016 by
GINNINDERRA PRESS
PO Box 3461 Port Adelaide 5015 Australia
www.ginninderrapress.com.au

Contents

Castles	9
This House of Stone	11
Narcissus	13
The Hare in the Moon	14
The Trout	15
Alouette	16
Lyrical Cat	17
Remembrance Day	18
Hopeful	19
A Memory of Stars	20
On Holdfast Bay	22
Fallow Land	23
I Would Be Ruled	24
Identity Crisis	25
The Sting	26
A Time for Joy	27
The Causeway	28
The Almond Trees	29
Foxes	31
Seeking for Truth	35
The Boy and Gunkar Singh	36
The Ship Carvers	38
A Mother's Lament	39
Attention Span	40
Grandma! Grandma!	41
Pigface	42
Pigface	43
Presence	44
Obsidian Darkness	45
Lost in Translation	46

The Execution	47
The Web	48
The Present	49
The Song	50
Selective Memory	53
Bluebell Woods	54
The Fawn	56
Ash Tree Nymphs	57
Memory Lane	58
The Rape of Mother Earth	60
The Whale Dreaming	61
Pressed Flowers	63
Homesickness	64
The Cruise Ship	65
Tell me a tale	66
The Dream	67
Moving Forward	70
Unfulfilled Promise	71
The Mirror	72
Butterflies	73
The Philosopher's Stone	74
The Conductor	75
Fine Art Photography	78
South Australian Summer	79
What is Holding up the Moon?	81
The Naked Lady	82
A One-night Stand	83
The Prado	84
To Cata	85
The Tour Down Under	86
The Diners	87
The Madrileña	88

The Artist	89
The Cuckoos	90
Unwritten Poetry	91
The Road to Salamanca	92
The Depths	93
The Traveller	94
Talking Turkey	95
The Scream	97
The Lesson	98
Pablito in Madrid	99
The Invitation	100
The Sceptic	101
The Cuckold	102
Spenser's Sonnets Unspencered	103
Dolphins	104
The Widow	105
Fleas	106
Written in Cobwebs	108
Huge the Hurt	110
Time Travel	111
The Clock	112
Ego	113

For my wonderful wife, Wendy
my inspirational children, Russell and Anna
and my beautiful new granddaughter, Teagan (#poet)

Castles

When I, as a boy, built castles,
I built them in the sand,
with seaweed flags and soaring spires,
and crenellations grand.

The ditch I dug became a moat;
waves wallowed all around.
When ramparts fell, my work decayed;
my castles were unsound.

This faceless boy confronts the storm,
too young to feed on dread.
His only shelter from the gale,
the bucket on his head.

His bucket has a hole in it;
it only holds the air.
His castles are intangible,
ethereal and rare.

These imaginary castles
are made of dreams and hope.
He has no tools with which to build –
the poor make do and cope.

Some build their castles in the sand,
and others in the air.
More solid castles do exist,
but such great works I fear,

for they were built by ruthless men
with rocks and iron bars,
depriving men of dreams and hope,
each day eclipsing stars.

This House of Stone

Blank verse

This house is strong with strength of stone, hand hewn
from slopes that sleep nearby; a silent gorge,
rock gouged. Such grants of life its settlers won.
Each stone was cut, its place in mind. Solid
were those that builded here, pragmatic men.

They had their dreams. Did they not sail across
the world in hope? Intrepid too, they stood
as proud as sun-drenched bluestone blocks they raised
to lock the years away while growing old.

Brooklands, thus built, those years ago, still stands
in place, aloof between a thirst of creeks
too weak to reach the sea, now dammed above
by greed; its livelihood withheld anon.

We bought this house, or rather it bought us.
It took on loan our lives, in trust that we
would care for it as others had before.
Its promise? Peace, blue wrens and silent hiss
of snakes to counterbalance Paradise.
We need to clothe ourselves in search of truth.

We too have built, in transit left our mark,
improving Nature's work with half an eye
upon our place in time. We seek to change
this land we call our own with pride. It's not,
for ownership lies on a road to hell,
and takes us there. Our efforts are in vain.
Ozymandian hopes soon turn to dust,
at best, we leave our spirit in this place.
Our days are brief. We sometimes look too far.

Narcissus

A heroic rispetto

In silence peril lies. The heart's forlorn
when apricot desires through shadows stray.
The harlequin who hesitates wins scorn,
for April's blossom cannot brook delay.

He wanders listlessly to azure pools,
the shaded depths of poesy and fools,
where blush the damask ripples of the moon
on images of self that seal his doom.

The Hare in the Moon

A sonnet

We seek for bounty on this earth so rare,
this perfect bubble in eternity,
as did the Buddha's incarnation, Hare,
sent out in vain for food. Though scarcity

denied his quest and earth could not provide,
he fed the whim of Indra, beggar Lord,
with his own flesh. The god was satisfied;
Hare's immortality was thus assured.

He now regards the ape and fox below
from his new home 'mid shadows on the moon,
returning balance to the tidal flow,
with calm, like notes upon a night bassoon,

whose mournful tones remind men that the price
of harmony is often sacrifice.

The Trout

A blank verse sonnet

Adrift upon the stream I drowned in thought
and did not see the gentle breeze spring up
to tease small mirrored clouds in stately dance
upon the ripple waves, as if afloat.
It tugged the autumn leaves and set them free;
released in death, they spun with joy and swirled.
These bobbing elfin craft, so pert and frail,
disturbed a rainbow wraith that lurked beneath.
Its sudden leap, with gormless maw agape,
unleashed a sun-drenched shower of crystal stars
that stopped my heart. Its beauty caught in time
remains with me. Such treasures buried deep
cannot be thieved, and form a precious store
to warm the sullen winter with their glow.

Alouette

Lest truth may be heard,
pluck quills from the bird
to keep the words from the wing,
but songs have a life
beyond all the strife,
and hearts that are free still sing.

Clip wings of the child
lest he become wild
and sing the songs of the free.
Bend him to your lies,
but still the song flies
with truth, that all men may see.

A deep oubliette
won't make men forget
the skies that once held a lark,
for evil can't quell
the musical swell
of tunes that banish the dark.

Lyrical Cat

Lyrical cat arched her back,
rubbed against my knee
seeking attention
so insistently
that I relented,
knowing full well that
stroking's essential
if one is going to maximise
purring potential.

Lyrical cats have sharp claws
and one thing's certain;
without attention
it can be curtains,
or at least egos
shredded. It takes grip
if one is going to maximise
a relationship

with lyrical cats. I know.
I was owned by one
a long time ago.
She lay in the sun
with one eye open,
knowing full well that
if one is going to maximise
life, one needs a cat.

Remembrance Day

Blank verse

A pallid light demystifies this dawn
but not the cause of war. The silence loud,
the sky is bruised with blood of those who fought
and died. I feel the chill of vapoured death
that dampens names engraved upon the cross
on this cold morn, as we remember them,
the serried ranks entrenched against their fear.
My father's Croix de Guerre upon my chest,
I struggle to remember him, again
constructing tales from silences inferred,
for these were days of which he never spoke.
He wore them though, upon his shadowed brow
and in his eyes, when badinage could not
conceal those deeper wounds of muddied brown,
the memories of war, that final war
to end all wars, they said. He wished it so.

Hopeful

A word acrostic

Hard-up in all except his youth, competitors were few,
Old men he spurned, their ways o'erturned, and thus his
    wealth soon grew.
'Person of power', they glibly said, and he believed it true.
Expecting all would honour him, he spent quadruple-fold,
Full of strength till age caught up; he then became less bold.
Useful limbs now turned to rust, and much to his dismay,
Life spent and fortune squandered, he found he'd had his day.

A Memory of Stars

The melting frost of night
entraps a star
within its universe,
a minuscule meniscus
that holds life
condensed from air,

whose warm caresses lifted it
from ocean depths,
redeemed from salty residues,
in feldspar caves

where crabs stalk sideways,
aslant from fear,
avoiding hidden vortices
that suck and blow
a rhythmic dance
on graves of conquistadors
dethroned; doublooned away
in shifting sand.

Clownfish and anemones
stand selfish guard, like misers,
protecting feeble glints of gold,
as lampreys slither through
the silent empty orbs,
In place of rotting flesh.

What impact made this sea;
this grave, awash with mariners
and vanished, murdered souls?

What vengeful god did seize,
and cast the catastrophic comet,
containing teratonnes of ice
to tilt our worldly axis,
making life –
a melt of tiny droplets
that hold a memory of stars,
from whence they came?

Minds were also made,
to thirst and reel
across the celluloid of life,
a passing dream,
a damp, pulsating fantasy
of dance within
a plasma skin of tension,
clinging, lest its star
should melt away,
returning home again.

On Holdfast Bay

An octogram

On Holdfast Bay, a sprightly craft
with lightsome breeze
will skim the waves. When wind's abaft;
enough to tease
and fill the sails, with skill I ply
a gull-wing course to make us fly.
I crave such days upon the seas
with lightsome breeze.

The price? Six days of grind and graft;
a boss to please,
whose red ink spoils my umpteenth draft.
More wasted trees!
With dread I view my office tray,
then dream a gust blows all away,
and thus my graft's dispelled and flees,
with lightsome breeze.

Fallow Land

The pessimist has furrows on his brow,
wherein a crop of worry seeds are sown,
and fertilised with fevered thoughts of doom.
He waters them with fear, a seeping damp,
and tends them with the burden of his care.

He makes the seedlings grow, and he predicts
them bio-engineered like Triffid spawn,
but they are all imaginings. Their crop,
ploughed back, will rot, providing compost fears
on fallow land, for him to sow again.
In this alone he is the optimist.

I Would Be Ruled

A kyrielle sonnet

I would be ruled by those who smile
at all their dreams, and reconcile
themselves to life, a lapsed ideal,
and concentrate on what is real.

I fear when passion holds the rein,
sustained by gods who feed on pain.
Such gods, if true, should surely heal
and concentrate on what is real.

May all our leaders love this earth,
beguiled by what it's really worth.
May they feel wonder, not just zeal,
and concentrate on what is real.

I would be ruled by those who smile
and concentrate on what is real.

Identity Crisis

A minute poem

We each are whole, but incomplete
till our minds meet
in riptide swell
of lovers' hell.

One half of self, subsumed to make
this strange retake,
shows mated gains,
yet there remains

a jagged cut to scar the face,
when we displace
our own designs
with lockstep lines.

The Sting

I'd been away in drunken flight,
side-slipping, sipping, life carousing,
strewing gardens with delight,
wings spread in sunshine, softly drowsing,
you espousing,
as I lingered, drinking light,
out of sight,

thinking you would come to me,
with your swaying lovers' hips
tempting thus the humble bee
to light upon the labial lips,
taking sips
of honeyed dreams, upon a sea
of ecstasy.

Yet you took a different pathway,
spreading stamens of desire
when you heard another voice pray
with subtle tempting words of fire.
He was a liar
when he plucked you from the clay
to have his way.

Too late I came upon that placement
where you lay drooping, as I found,
behind a flyblown cottage casement,
petals falling on the ground
without a sound
to signify the sad abasement
your cutting lent.

A Time for Joy

A villanelle

These triplet lambs of late were born.
Their life is blessed, but may be short;
a time for joy, a time to mourn.

Their mother's udder is foresworn;
they try to suck and then abort.
These triplet lambs of late were born.

The Paschal Lamb from us was torn.
He gave His life but not for naught.
A time for joy, a time to mourn.

We pray our lambs may see the dawn
And, by His grace, in fields cavort;
These triplet lambs of late were born.

Ewe's expressed milk they do not scorn;
it gives them strength - a last resort.
A time for joy, a time to mourn.

She shuns them now the bond is shorn;
our intervention lacks support.
These triplet lambs of late were born.
A time for joy, a time to mourn.

The Causeway

A sonnet

Some days I stand beyond myself and see,
through swirling mists, a destination sought;
an island split from mainland certainty
by seas that isolate my every thought.

This island is myself – a no-man's-land
between the warring elements of doubt
and faith – a granite outcrop in the sand
that builds a bar to keep intruders out.

Perhaps a causeway could be built between
the mainland mass and island Mandelbrot
that splits the fractal essence from obscene
routines of daily life, and one that's got

the screwpile jetty strength to span my mind
with planks to join my dreams to all mankind.

The Almond Trees

Blank verse

These trees aligned upon the eastern slope
extend arthritic arms towards the dawn
their blackened limbs bend painfully to catch
each warming ray, to dry the dew from webs
that wove their silver strands in birds' nest hair.
Ten years ago I nearly cut them down
to make way – but make way for what? Too steep
for pickers now, who like more even ground,
where iron claws can take indecent grip
to shake the almonds off and half the leaves.

I thought the trees no good, they'd had their day,
but then the blossoms came, a few at first,
small vanities of age, quite shyly worn
unlike the bloom of youth's fecundity.
Our orchard bears the promise of lush fruit,
the nubile pear and peach and cherry lips
in Spring, but these nine trees will case their gifts
in green, a cloak to hide their bitterness.

Their broken limbs a scratching post for kine,
reveal a cleft, for native bees a home,
whose oozing sweet abundance tempts a pair
of yellow honey eaters to enjoy
an amber feast warmed by the winter sun.
They also have their place upon the hill
to cheer the hearts of lovers down below,
who honeymoon in winter by the fire,
and kindle caves of passion in its flames.

The gardens waft their narcissistic scents
Of lavender for bees and jonquil bulbs,
germander blue and ornamental quince,
and overlooking all…these almond eyes.

When summer comes, a host of cockatoos
will flash their yellow tails and swoop and screech,
descending once again to ravage them,
yet they will survive. Bushfires burnt the farm
in '59 but only charred their trunks.
I've grown to like their lovely uselessness;
their stand in face of failing life and age.

Foxes

Pause of russet red,
Mistrust, a pricked up ear,
on either side abated breath.
I stood still,
poised on heron stalks,
as they resumed their play,
a dainty rough and tumble on the hill,
with sun-flecked blazes, white
from russet torn,
like tardy feathers from the poultry pen,
the habit of my mind connecting
foxes with foul play.
Where was my gun?

and yet…
I have no fowls,
no argument with foxes,
no need to stop the clock
with puff of scattered lead,
the seeds of war,

in case they stole imagined hens;
no cause to kill for sport
like foxes do
in frenzied genocide.

Last spring a snake upreared
to strike me down,
and changed its mind
Would I have stayed my hand?

The cubs seemed not to fear;
perhaps they knew
I owned the bramble patch
that harboured them,
a home
so handy to br'er rabbit's hole,
wood ducks upon the dam,
and small birds,
condemned to watchfulness
and darting, fearful flight
from bush to briar rose,
aware of blackness buried
at the heart of things.

I stood still
as did the hawk,
balanced on a barely quivering wing,
side-slipping air
before he wheeled away,
attracted by a native hopping mouse
whose day was done.

Last night I dreamt of death and heard a howl,
an eerie banshee wail upon the hill.
A vixen stood and faced
the pallid roundness of a hunter's moon
that spilled a glint of blue
into her keening cry.
Why such utter grief?
My heart went cold.

Today
the sun was shining.
My cottage guests
remarked,
'There is a fox.'
'Two,' I said,
'I saw them play.'
'Just one,'
they said,
'a cub,
curled in sleep
beside the crazy paving path.
Come and see.'

How peaceful seemed the hand of death,
head lolling in the languid grass,
eyes closed;
no sign of miles
dragged home
in misery here,
of poisoned bile and retch,
to reach this resting place,
this final sanctuary.

I picked him gently up,
blood dripped on feet of clay.
I took him down the hill,
and placed him on a funeral pyre
of boxthorn and of life's debris,
athwart the chicken coop
we do not use
for fear of foxes,
and I watched again,
as smoke curled slow away.

Seeking for Truth

A fusion sonnet

Seeking for truth, men delve in the past,
read words from dead scrolls, drown in green waste,
tear flesh from the gods, gnawing their bones. A bitter taste
taints underworld cups, with venom well laced.
Poison drains from their minds, that seeped from the past,
where dogma was found. Wearing robes of the night,
false priests poise their knives…to blight
the children we bear, blinding their sight.
'How long must this last?
How long?' good men ask.

Seas can support and keep us afloat,
so why should we drown in wrecks cast upon rocks?
We may hold our course steady, avoiding the crash,
if we hold out our hands to those who are lost

seeking for truth. Men delve in the past,
and buoyed up by learning, add wisdom to life,
unless mired in the depths of sectarian strife.
When men keep to the surface where breezes hold sway
filling their sails, enjoying each day
skimming the waves, with their eyes on the mast,
poison drains from their minds, that seeped from the past.

The Boy and Gunkar Singh

Blank verse

A small boy wandered free, the sahib's son.
The world was his, because the tropic noon
had driven men indoors and under fans
to sip their cooling gins and talk. They spoke,
elastic fervour hiding their intent
regarding rubber futures and the yield
of latex, caught in sticky copra cups
by coolies under conic bamboo hats.

Meanwhile, their women played at bridge and trumped
each other's conquests, playing jacks and kings
with reputations, laughingly with barbs
that wounded prettily, on pouting lips.

Each day he slipped across the cow-grass lawns,
touched mimosa leaves and made them close
with potent magic, not yet understood,
and crushed the purple powder puffs of flowers
unthinkingly beneath his suntanned toes,
as on he strode, towards the marble steps
where Gunkar Singh, the splendid Sikh, stood guard
and welcomed members of the country club,
with haughty, regal mien.

'Sat Shri Akal,'
he greeted him; in truth, God reigns supreme.
'Sat Shri Akal,' replied the sahib boy,
for he had learnt to speak with courtesy.
He loved that man, whose eyes were deepest pools
of Eastern fire beneath his bushy brows,
whose grey, free-flowing beard and whiskers waxed
around his fiery mouth, a dragon's cave
of betel juice and alabaster teeth.
'Sit down, sahib, seek rest from noonday heat.'

… And so he sat, spellbound by Punjab tales,
absorbing culture in his growing mind,
until in time he grew to be a man
beyond the wit of those whose rubber cheques
erased dull brains with juniper, within.

The Ship Carvers

Blank verse

I wandered down the dusty sun-dried streets;
paint peeled like skin. Verandas lurched and swayed
like drunks, upheld by women at the door,
lest they should fall and bring the washing down.
Lianas spanned the gaps with easy grace,
while flaunting torrid colours, reds and blues,
amongst the faded skirts. Some kiskadees,
consuming lice, fell silent as I passed.

Beyond this squalor stood a house on stilts,
whose shadow blocked the unforgiving sun
to shade a boy intent on whittling wood.
His gap-toothed grin invited me to pause
and watch, for in the shadows others lazed
with wood between their knees or on their laps
and carved, releasing shapes that leapt in flight
before a sultry wind. A sloop was born
that day; each member of this family,
according to his skill with whetted knife,
unmade the crooked grain of hardship's toil
and shaved the sullen wood till sails unfurled.

I turned, retracing steps to tourist haunts,
where people haggle for their souvenirs
with misanthropic meanness, 'spite of means,
before re-boarding well-heeled sailing ships
to cross the gulf, and set a course for home,
resuming crooked paths of venal gain,
their sloops becalmed upon the mantelshelf.

A Mother's Lament

Where shall I journey now my boy is gone,
for I am left in limbo, lost, forlorn?
The drum no longer beats. The fife's at rest,
and March winds mock a mother's withered breast.
Now beating through the formless night till dawn,
they drive the dust like tears as yet unborn.
Where shall I journey now my boy is gone?
My boy is gone.

My footsteps turn to tread the path of blame,
for he was filled with images of fame
by jingoistic calls to join the fight
for freedom and for glory and for right.
You promised you would honour my child's name.
Posthumous decoration's not the same.
My footsteps turn to tread the path of blame,
the path of blame.

The echoes of the wind that blow
breathe softly…silent whispers.
Perchance you hear the heart's blood flow
while kneeling at your vespers.
The ground is hallowed where you tread.
His footprints near the river bed
were stained with russet where he bled.
Should I forgive your trespass?

Attention Span

A ballade

Quantum physics says I shall cease to be
should you decide to shift your loving gaze
and turn your eyes elsewhere, away from me;
You have it in your power to end my days.
My love for you is not a passing phase;
Have pity on this foolish moonstruck man.
Oh, how I love you! I am lost in praise!
My future lies in your attention span.

Though I'm enchained, your eyes can set me free
to live a life of bliss. My fancy plays
with cheerful thoughts of domesticity
with you, my love, my life, my only craze.
I offer you the world! Attention pays
when such an offer's made. I'm rich. I can
bestow great wealth, so if you're wise, appraise…
Your future lies in your attention span.

There is another side to this! You see,
if my attention lapses and eyes glaze
when foolish tantrums make us disagree,
you'll find that quantum physics works both ways.
I glance away and you become a phrase
deleted from my life. Our blissful plan
will slip its sheets, adrift from loosened stays.
Your future lies in my attention span.

How quickly love unravels. When it frays
for lack of caring love, as it sure can,
thoughts each for other reignite the blaze.
Our future lies in our attention span.

Grandma! Grandma!

A rondeau redouble

'Grandma! Grandma!' the young girl cried,
clutching her cape, spattered with red;
a hollow shell, empty inside,
but for the waves that crashed in her head.

The rubble-filled streets filled her with dread;
her home was erased, no place to hide;
there beneath bricks her grandma lay dead.
'Grandma! Grandma!' the young girl cried.

Raped by soldiers roughly astride,
robbed of her childhood, obscenely spread,
their lust sated, her ropes were untied.
Clutching her cape, spattered with red,

she crept away, footsteps like lead,
filled with shame, with no-one to guide,
staggering south, aimless she fled;
a hollow shell, empty inside

except for accretions of pride
to turn to the world when she bled
from a past she could have denied
but for the waves that crashed in her head,

for flashbacks are easily fed
by chance. Just today she espied
a girl with a seashell, who sped
up the beach, and with laughter cried,
'Grandma! Grandma!'

Pigface

(June)

Its common name is pigface. Why, I do not know.
I gouged a hole and stuck it in, with hopes that it might grow.
Clay and shale the rock face, steep unforgiving land.
Our other plants were put to bed in compost, loam and sand.
The embryonic pigface was buried when it rained.
Silt ran down upon it; one single leaf remained.

The sun cased that in concrete; at least I thought it so.
I shrugged and gave up on it, sure it could not grow.
But pig was a survivor and now it's spreading down,
Clinging most tenaciously, and rooting in new ground.
Each leaf a pudgy thumb of juice, with crimson stars to come,
Its leaves conserve the moisture to stand the summer's sun.

Our other plants are whingeing about the winter weeds;
I haven't time to tend to them or nurture all their needs.
Without water they will wither, these namby-pamby plants,
I swear they're more demanding than a score of maiden aunts.
I raise my hat to pigface with its pudgy little thumbs,
For here's an Aussie battler that will take whatever comes.

Pigface

(November)

Its common name is pigface. I told you so in June.
Since then it's gone on spreading and is halfway down the dune,
beyond the town of Goolwa, towards the Murray mouth.
Our little garden monster is also heading south.
It's stretched its pudgy fingers into fissures in the rock
exploring all around it, like a child that's reared on Spock.

Now that spring is with us, it's coming into bloom.
With a common name like pigface one might easily assume
it would be rather ugly, but that is not the case.
Children often bully, using features of the face,
to win their peers' approval, with a cruel and hurtful name.
A kid called Carpobrotus would sure attract their aim!

When the sun is shining brightly it blossoms with a smile,
but if dark clouds are looming it closes down awhile.
It's just the same with children, when feeling safe and warm
they open up delightfully, but not when there's a storm.
Our pigface is a battler and is sure to win (with praise),
but some other butts of bullies are scarred for all their days.

Presence

A blank verse sonnet

The sounds that come from silence fill the void
between the stars. Shut down your mind, be still
and let them in. The song of nightingales,
Death's tuneful whippoorwill…may both be heard,

for notes ascend in grief as well as joy.
A pause in life will cheat the clock of time;
expand this fragment of eternity
to play your tune, and make its vibrance felt.

Alone, the wain will wend a rutted path,
its destination known, by nightmares drawn.
Unharness them from your accreted load
and let them go. Embrace each moment now.

The past is but a slideshow of the mind;
and future gains…? May not be yours to own.

Obsidian Darkness

A triversen (after William Carlos Williams)

Obsidian glass
sets in the lava floor;
a prison of darkness.

Life's brief light,
encased in a mirror,
now looks inward.

There lies within this polished tomb
the cutting edge of hope,
or is it fear?

Enough to overturn a mind
with blind volcanic sparks
of released emotion.

The glazing rush of heat
makes solid scalpel sharpness
for a surgical incision.

A pendant jewel swings
at the victim's throat,
reflecting a lost city.

Lost in Translation

A triolet

How much is lost when we translate?

Our soaring thoughts in static words
are, at their best, but second-rate.

How much is lost, when we translate
small joys we would articulate,
like whirring wings of hummingbirds.

How much is lost when we translate
our soaring thoughts in static words!

The Execution

A sanguine glow seeps through the crack of dawn.
Two men now face this fissure in the sky
behind the firing squad. The beads are drawn,
sweat dampens as a dew. They're bound to die,

for their dark crime. Some murders men condone,
a simple retribution, eye for eye,
meted without mercy; the first stone thrown
by righteous men who set themselves on high.

A staccato volley sounds, like applause
to greet the bloodstained weals that bruise the sky.
This firmament of justice has its flaws;
whose are the bleeding hearts as these men die?

The Web

A blank verse sonnet

A gossamer of droplets caught the sun
in rainbow pendants. They hung, glistening
like quiet tears of joy to greet the dawn;
a shimmering suspension, bridging fear.

Then – vibrato! The morning came to life.
A small wren swept in, landing with a lurch.
The sedge sagged low, but gave to hold his weight.
He shook a crystal shower where pearls had been,

then off he flew. The web was set once more,
an unseen danger now between two blades
and in the sawfly sailed unwittingly
to spring the sticky trap spun in the night

In beauty entangled, it writhed in vain;
the arachnid ambled out to eat her prey.

The Present

I am here, alone, in this moment
centred in a circularity
that has neither beginning nor end,
in a space that lies beyond belief.
I deny the pale ghosts of the past
and the future, as I fall out of time
like a child, unwrapping the present.

The Song

Blank verse

The woman wandered through the trees with thoughts
of her new child, the one she now conceived
in her mind's eye. She lay beside a brook
that babbled in its play. A song arose
with resonance that filled her empty womb.
Its swelling sound and lithesome curves took shape,
like water ever wending ocean bound;
a journey we all make with blood that ebbs
according to a rhythm preordained.
She softly sang the notes that came to mind,
composed of love, for she would wake the babe
with this, his song. His time would soon arrive.

She waited like Rebekah at the well
to find the father of the child to come.
Skilled notes she wove to catch a conjoint heart
to share with hers, in love to make the child,
enchanted by her embryonic tune.
At length he came to quench his thirst and hers;
the music of their love profoundly moved
all those who heard their song, for from their love
new life would spring; a boy, a destiny
sublime; a boy – in short – who knew his song.
Oh, blessed indeed, for some are out of tune
and spend frenetic lives in harsh discord.

What joy, what celebration, what soft tears
accompanied the birth. In unison,
combined in single voice, the village sang
encouragement to help the new child through
his clouded days, for life's more shadowed hours
are bleak when faced without support, bereft
of those who care. To raise a child it takes
a whole community with just one aim;
to save him from himself in times of need.
Thus strong in strength of love the man matured,
protected by the breadth of this great shield
until at last it was his time to leave

for war, as most young men will do to save
what they hold dear; for some, a war of words,
for others, strife on foreign soil with blood
and comradeship, close knit by circumstance.
It was his lot to fight a soldier's war,
entrenched against young men he did not know
how best to hate. In those dark days he taught
his song to mates who had not learnt to sing
their childhood dreams. The words defied disease,
cold steel, their fear and endless misery.
He shared his song that they might own its worth
before their lives were torn apart by guns.

He drifted back, a broken, shell-shocked man,
without the means to override the moans
whose tuneless monotone drowned out his sense
of self. His mother's voice, though cracked and old,
still keened to comfort him, his father's too,
and all who held him dear. In course of time,
with patient love, they nursed him back to health
until when passing by the well one day
he chanced to hear a teasing, lilting air
he recognised. He was made whole again
by limpid notes and a beguiling smile,
and his grey geese took flight and disappeared.

Selective Memory

In this still world of silence, I am not
alone. I have a tale of years
to pin upon my brazen chest, suborned
to be sublime in this, my afterglow.

My vagaries disport like firelight wraiths,
half seen in reveries of misted sight.

The rhythm of my heart is in my words.
Though these be bound within a metric cage,
they tug like tattered flags against the wind,
defying chains of rhyme-imprisoned verse.

I would that you could hear their siren call
within these ink-dried pages, vellum-bound.

Poor judgement sealed their sentence long ago.
Their cell should resonate with deeper chords,
whose soft vibrations haunt my ears alone,
so wrapped in contexts that cannot be shared.

I hear them loud, as in the days of old,
but feel them gently as in Blind Man's Buff.

They tease my failing senses as I stretch
to touch the past again, relive its joys,
recalling famous deeds from distant youth,
well censored by selective memory,

a childish game to hide the wayward tracks
of older men, and sweeten words to mask

the bitter aftertaste of life's dark days.
We choose the honeyed moments to retell.

Bluebell Woods

A blank verse sonnet sequence

A small shy boy, an art shed in a school,
a dream that floated in the burnished dust
of sunlight, shifting through the swaying leaves.
He took a brush, blue paint, and with his heart

he daubed. Although quite tentative at first,
his mind created pixie-laden shapes
of flowers – faerie bells with nodding heads.
Then tempted by his palette's colour range

his mingled paints became an earthy brown.
with which he grew amazing twisted trees,
a darkling wood of dangers yet untold
and there among the faerie folk he went.

The brush-strokes of his mind had captured him;
his heart was ransomed to his bluebell woods.

*

To bluebell woods each spring his heart was drawn,
Their heady perfume acted like a drug
to feed his growing love of solitude
In sylvan shades. Distrust of people grew,

and he would covet secret dells and brakes,
imagining that they were his alone,
but then he met a girl who – sighing – swooned
into his arms. In dalliance they wove

twin garlands of the woodland hyacinth
that tied them to their truth, in ancient lore,
and thus adorned, these lovers plighted troth.
At last he'd found someone with whom to share.

His bluebell woods gained magic, for her hold
on him enriched the palette of his dreams

*

In bliss they trod the byways of their youth
without a care for life's vicissitudes.
until one day, disporting in a glade,
a jealous wind arose and broke a branch

which crashed upon the love he held so close.
Her body crushed the fragile faerie bells.
Benumbed, he clasped her hand and watched her go,
as lifeblood seeped into the soft brown earth

He was distraught and stumbled in his grief,
while shedding bitter tears upon the flowers,
as, long ago, Apollo too had done,
whose discus felled his lover, Hyacinth.

Thus history repeats, for jealous winds
whip up, when we approach too close to heaven.

The Fawn

There's stillness in the glen,
no breath of wind to stir
the mists that hide the vale
at dawn. Yet if there were

a breeze, I'd waken her
and whisper to the dawn
to warm the frozen rill,
to tempt the timid fawn,

caress with pale sunrise
her twitching upright ear,
with creeping warmth assail
the prison of her fear.

There's stillness in the glen
as she walks down the hill
with dainty careful steps.
at length to drink her fill

Ash Tree Nymphs

A sonnet

A single drop of blood proved seminal
in spawning Ash Tree Nymphs, a honeyed breed
who, like all dryads, are ephemeral
as breaths of air that waft the wingèd seed

to form new forests on this precious earth.
They also reared Olympus's highest lord,
and danced and sang with Pan in joyful mirth,
free spirits all, in ancient times adored,

but now we have lost touch. Each tree we fell
cuts off a dryad's breath. When they are gone,
this paradise is lost in which we dwell,
and then, I fear, 'twill be too late to mourn.

The god of air's castration by his son
was nought, compared with what mankind's undone.

Memory Lane

In days gone by, a bridle track
ran past the place where we were wed.
Reflective moments take me back
to this idyll – a watershed.

My heart recalls our Wiltshire lane
at break of day. I loved that place.
I walk it in my mind again.
An early dew on Queen Anne lace

reflects the sun's candescent light.
Haphazard leggy stalks now stretch
above the verge of fading night,
their fragile hoods of purple vetch

like butterflies, while down beneath,
the speedwell shyly hides its flowers,
from all but knowing eyes. Its wreath
of blue lies soft in mossy bowers.

A scent of hawthorn fills the air.
The finch chirrups his cheerful song,
a fleeting tune. He pauses here,
upon a catkin twig – then gone.

The sun now bathes the fescue field,
with buttercup and dandelion,
that guards the boundary of the weald,
which lies beyond. I have my eye on

the margin of this pheasant wood,
a mile or so from Castle Combe,
where Max let slip he'd seen some good
morels that grew in umber loam.

I covet them, though when first seen
their conic brains most surely must
defy all thoughts of haute cuisine;
their convolutions cause disgust.

When thinly sliced and seared with heat,
in butter from the Jersey herd,
there is no finer fungal treat,
not even truffles! Mark my word!

We cut a few but leave the rest
for others yet to come, with whom
we share this hamlet, heaven-blest,
for greed, I fear, is friendship's doom.

The friends we made in those far days
remain with us down through the years.
Some now are dead, but friendship stays
in memory…and private tears.

The Rape of Mother Earth

Blank verse

How good this earth! How blessèd is the soil
and they who husband it. How wise were those
who called her Mother Earth, for she, in truth,
does succour us and feed her children well.

The ancients knew to sacrifice to Gaia
and flatter her with gifts to make her sweet.
Her skin is not so thick as it appears
when children fail in filial respect,

and yet, I fear, we now forget ourselves
in yielding to the deadly sin of greed.
We scarify her skin with deep-cut ploughs;
like Cadmus then, we sow the dragon's teeth.

Monsanto, do you hear the goddess howl?
Are we now gods to engineer our gain?
Did Sodom suck the ancient dugs till dry?
Gomorrah sinned but mothers were not raped.

The gods are quick to anger, so beware.
Aeolus will unleash his savage winds
to lift our Mother into Neptune's arms.
Soon she'll desert us, for the sands of time.

The Whale Dreaming

Alliterative verse

This Dreaming relates the doom of Kondoli,
who carried the flame… Fire flew from his feet
inciting envy amongst enemies,
tempting Tiritpa and his friend Tjintrin
to take his tinder by an act of treachery,
despicably stealing the sacred spark.

A party was planned, promising people
dancing and delight as darkness descended.
According to custom, Kondoli came
bringing warmth against winter.

With sudden surprise the saboteurs sprang
from behind bushes that shaded the beach,
striking savagely with sharpened spears,
piercing his neck with their points, painfully.

Sparks sizzled, cartwheeled and spun
as he leapt in alarm loosing leviathan,
spouting water from his weeping wound,
then, becoming as one with the wandering whale,
he sank slowly, subsumed by the sea.

His friends followed, forgoing the form
of mere mortals, they mutated in misery,
to become Kondoli's constant companions:
the savage shark, the stingray and seal.

Tiritpa and Tjintrin were also transformed;
the fire they fomented forced them to fly,
forestalled and forever foregoing the flame.

One became wagtail, a woebegone bird,
fitfully flitting, an object of fun,
while a dirge of despond to this day can be heard
from his lilting accomplice, a spiralling lark.

Pressed Flowers

A villanelle

Forgotten flowers from the fields and coast,
estranged reminders of a love askew,
are pressed within this letter I'll not post.

Each petal lies as silent as a ghost,
a haunted past, when swallows overflew
forgotten flowers from the fields and coast.

Frail desiccated blooms – dry as our boast
of faithfulness that sparkled in the dew –
are pressed within this letter I'll not post.

Well watered by regret, they live – almost,
but then they fade. Once more just jaded blue
forgotten flowers from the fields and coast,

that waved awhile, a gay and joyful host
along our way. Regrets at losing you
are pressed within this letter I'll not post,

so let me now propose a maudlin toast
to drown the memory of our love, once true.
Forgotten flowers from the fields and coast
are pressed within this letter I'll not post.

Homesickness

I speak in foreign tongues tonight
to make you understand
that this is not my land,
although my life is here.

I weep with silent tears tonight;
their swell submerges me.
I sail a drowning sea
that calls to me from there.

My home is in my dreams tonight
but where, I cannot say,
for I have lost my way,
and life slips by, I fear.

The echo of my home tonight
hangs soft upon the air.
With each departing year,
this echo rings less clear.

I dream I'm coming home tonight.
Although my life is here,
I drift and disappear
in thoughts too hard to share.

The Cruise Ship

She sidled in from out at sea,
her cargo, sloth and apathy
lounging listless, languidly.

I guessed three thousand by her size
suspended 'twixt the sea and skies,
ample bosoms, sun-burned thighs,

men to match, with their pot-bellies,
over-spilling shorts like jellies.
Is this heaven, or what hell is?

The palm-fringed beach is swept clean
by native men, bronzed and lean;
a contrast some might find obscene.

Tell me a tale

Tell me a tale. Sing me a song
Assault my tears. String me along.
Here is my heart. Quicken the beat
Capture my ears with your deceit.

Lead me a dance. Hang disbelief.
You are my time. Time is my thief
Sharpen my pen. Cut to the chase.
This is my life. You are its pace.

Massage my words. Let me enthuse.
This is my rhyme. You are my muse.
Sing me your soul, a song sublime.
Our tale will last while you are mine.

The Dream

Blank verse

So soft the dream in its becoming sigh,
a breath so slight its life was hard to see,
its darkness such as only night could form,
awaiting such new hope as day might bring.
The dream was small, its whisper just begun,
as when, cocooned in larval state, a moth
will struggle from the confines of its cell,
and spread its velvet wings to catch the glow
of moonlight spilt from ragged, winter veils.
Upon this journey, too, the dream would drift,
its wings unfurl, and waft into the air,
in search of truth, elusive as a ghost.

When high above a town, the moth soon met
his nemesis, a burning candlestick
that beckoned from an artist's attic space,
attracting him. Its snake-like flicker fell
upon an open casement's glinting glass
and mesmerised his mind, so in he flew
around the flame, that tempting promised land
that many seek when spilling stylus words,
intent upon impressing wax-filled ears.
In seeking truth, he came too close and died.

The artist paused to dip his brush in oil
while musing on the miracle of flight
and how to catch its essence in a line,
a vibrant shape, a blur of beating blades.
He turned to see the moth in melted wax,

like Icarus who ventured near the sun
and perished in the heat of his desire,
and yet, surviving death, a peacock's eye
regarded him from its dismembered wing,
a glint of hope that struggled to survive.
Inspired, he caught its spirit in the plane
that soared across the canvas of his work
for all the world to see in time, on show.

It chanced a boy walked by and paused awhile,
enraptured when he saw the artist's flight.
This was his dream; he clutched it near his heart
and took it home. In fear lest it escape,
he tied his captive down with loving care,
entailed upon a kite he sometimes launched,
but dreams are light and apt to drift away
with paper shapes that float against the wind,
unless they're firmly held. He tethered it
with silken thread to let it play, constrained
within the limits of his childish whim.
He fed it out, but only cautiously
before he reeled it in again, once more
to languish in his bedroom box of toys.
The dream lay still and waited for the hour
when it would freely fly. What joy it was
when, one fine day at last it soared
and chased a wayward wind. The boy ran too.
He strained against the string, and almost left
the ground that tethered him. With sudden sweeps
and dives, at length the fragile kite broke loose

and snapped the thread that bound it to the child.
It whirled and spun and tore itself to shreds,
as people do when zeal outruns intent.

The boy, bereft, began to climb the branch
to rescue remnants of his broken kite.
Just then a passing jay of vivid blue,
attracted by the ribboned tail that swung,
as does the fisher's fly on swirling pool,
alighted, snatched the prize with gleeful cry
and flew to line his nest with bunting, gay
as any found at fairs throughout the land,
then perched, to dream the flight of fledglings three.
The boy, amazed by beauty of the bird,
forgot his loss and dreamt he too might soar
in search of skies beyond the height of clouds,
for dreams don't die, although at times they pause
to seek expression through another mind.

Moving Forward

A pantoum

Four steps forward, two steps back,
The poet's dance from yesteryear,
Chained by echoes that I hear,
My brain is stretched upon the rack.

The poet's dance from yesteryear,
It stretches out, and then pulls back.
My brain is stretched upon the rack,
Moving on yet staying here,

It stretches out, and then pulls back.
Past is certain; progress, fear,
Moving on yet staying here.
It is, like truth, a slippery track.

Past is certain; progress, fear.
Chained by echoes that I hear.
It is, like truth, a slippery track;
Four steps forward, two steps back.

Unfulfilled Promise

A sonnet

I searched my heart and found it bound to Sue's.
Her strings, oh gee, were used to capture it.
Such love affairs are often caused by booze,
For cocktail bars can tempt one, tot by tit,

Enticing one to stand with due respect.
Good manners make the man, or so they say,
Though at my lessons I did not suspect
Correctness could effect such ecstasy.

Maintaining such erectness, gin by gin,
Was not so easy as it seemed to be.
At length, when Sue was wooed and let me in,
I found myself bereft of chivalry.

A knight with spirit gives a decent ride,
But sadly too much spirit was inside.

The Mirror

Mirror, mirror, on the floor,
leaning up beside the door,
your gilt surround
mocked mine,
you swine,
and so I took you down.

Butterflies

They flutter by
like sighs of love
with perfumed breath,
as when
your kiss is nigh
my love,
and then
they pause for nectar,
like you and I,
my butterfly.

The Philosopher's Stone

Today, once more, I play with words,
engaging alchemy of old.
With subterfuge of metaphor,
I seek to turn my lead to gold.

I capture sunlight with my pen,
mistaking its reflective glare
for treasure at the rainbow's end,
but rainbows' ends just disappear.

I roam in realms of fantasy
and there I hear a golden bird.
I fancy that my leaden verse
will also sing, but that's absurd.

Base metal in a crucible
was fired with hope in days of old,
as now I fire my tinpot words
with transubstantial dreams of gold.

The Conductor

A ripple rises as the lights are dimmed
that grows into a crescendo of applause.
The great man appears.
An emperor penguin,
he sweeps across the stage
and mounts the podium
then turns,
surveys his audience,
and nods acknowledgement.

The scene is set. His baton raised,
he holds expectant silence in the air,
then gently coaxes murmurs from the violins,
a rising susurration of bees set free.
He suppresses them
with a gentle downward movement of his hand,
turns his pointer to the larger deep-voiced strings,
demanding their masculine response,
an ominous drumbeat of rising sound
that enforces interplay with melody.
He draws music forth
with an outstretched hand.

The tempo quickens to the strident shudder of his jowl.
He turns a white-tipped laser to the centre of the pit.
It strikes, exploding brass, timpani and a kettledrum
before an opening bloom of cymbals
stops their breath.

Majestically, he cuts the air.
Great swathes of sound escape,
marshalled by his rhetoric into ranks.
His eye is wild, he leads the charge
as if on horseback,
the rise and fall of his shoulders
mimicked by a rippling surge
across the silken blackness of his back.
He cuts the sound away again,
severing its roots with silence.

A single flute dares defy him now.
It mourns the melody with keening liquid notes.
The maestro turns
and coaxes once again the strings,
drawing from their amber hearts
accompaniment,
a waterfall of sound
cascading from Olympian heights.

The final notes ascend.
They float like butterflies returning to the gods.
The audience erupts,
washing the magic away
in a torrent of sound.
He turns, bows low,
acknowledges the thunder of applause,
and then is gone.

The orchestra subsides
like puppets who have lost their puppeteer.
Exchanging pleasantries, they pack their bags for home.
The symphony is done.

Fine Art Photography

She calls it fine art when she cuts off heads.
We are left to imagine the teenage dreads,
suck face slurps of osculation,
and ardent sighs of acned frustration.

When lovers embrace in a public place,
invading the bounds of personal space,
they're easy targets for a street art lens
that can broadcast the lie of 'Just good friends'.

She shoots her victims who seem unaware
that dangers lie hidden everywhere.
Such private pleasures are best kept in beds;
there are jihadists, too, that cut off heads.

South Australian Summer

There is a stillness in the air,
a languid stillness
in which pendulous leaves
sway feebly
to catch each tepid breeze.

Two Adelaide rosellas swoop
from shade to nearby shade,
brief sparks of life
in the blue haze
of lazy afternoon.

An ancient red gum
sheds a swath of sunburnt skin,
revealing layers of whiteness
splotched with grey
indifference.

The sleepy lizard edges
gratefully
into the new-found shade
and shelters there,
waiting for the moon to bathe
such wounds of day
in silver.

Then shadows will awaken
and wide-eyed possums stare,
as small scavengers
scuttle-search for prey,
themselves reflected
in the amber eyes
of soft-winged spectres,
silent overhead.

What is Holding up the Moon?

You ask what's holding up the moon
above young lovers as they spoon
with silver tongues and mystery
and silken threads of poesy.

It's bound by strings from conjoint hearts
and held in place by Cupid's darts.
So long as we believe in love
our faith will keep the moon above.

Though science may refute my claim
I still believe it, just the same,
for love and faith and heartfelt hope
have always kept our dreams afloat.

The Naked Lady

A sonnet

This Naked Lady causes some surprise
when she unfurls herself from nature's bed,
and flaunts her perfect pinkness to the skies
while, teasingly, she nods her lovely head.

In '83 this land was seared by fire,
the dragon raged for days without respite,
all dreams of men were cast upon the pyre,
the ashen landscape held no hint of light,

but, three days on, a miracle occurred.
New life broke through the blackened forest floor
and clumps of perfect pinkness rose and stirred
a sense of hope – as Christ had done before.

These Resurrection Lilies vanquished death,
as Naked Ladies do, with teasing breath.

A One-night Stand

Night-scented trees
scattered moonlight
playfully
on white spider lilies
in a lavender hedge;
a virginal offering
for the soft grey moth
proffering sex.

Alas,
the harsh light of day
brought winds of change
that blew away their standing.

Now,
cut off in their prime,
they languish on the shelf,
still dreaming of the garden
but imprisoned by the pane.

The Prado

Blank verse

I stand before Madrid's most famous place.
Its gaping maw will soon consume a crowd
of tourists tempted, hooked on history,
and reeled into El Prado where they'll gawk
and swirl amid the best of Spanish art

in jeans, as Christ looks down with saddened eyes,
forgiving them. Oh, how the nobles sneer,
disdaining contact with this motley crew.
Prometheus endures the eagle who
destroys his liver day by day to warn
a mob of chicks who cluck, and peck at phones,
ignoring Rubens' classic masterpiece.

El Greco, Velasquez and others toiled;
their brush strokes matching might with misery
to entertain this intestinal hoard,
who swim amongst the entrails, hall by hall,
until at last it's closing time and then,
incontinent with age, El Prado shits
its tourist load upon the sunlit street.

They dribble down the steps. Siesta time,
so now the mighty monolith can sleep.

To Cata

A sonnet

The luscious berry's red, Desire its name.
It tastes obscenely fragrant, sugar-sweet.
I hold it on my tongue and feel no shame,
Enjoying aromatic, tropic heat.

A subtle scent of lemon fills my void;
It mingles soft with jasmine of the night;
The blackness is a sin to be enjoyed.
My senses quicken, heartbeat's out of sight,

For these ripe beans that rev me for my date
Were plucked from Costa Rica's highland slopes,
And ground with loving care to Number 8,
And as they plunged, they raised my ardent hopes.

I pray my girl is sparked with like desire;
Her coffee-coloured skin sets me on fire.

The Tour Down Under

A roundelay

Now begins the Tour Down Under
A world renowned cycle race.
It's a South Australian funder,
Mental test of heartbeat pace.
Each year I am stunned with wonder;
Hugging Lycra fills this place.

It's a South Australian funder,
Mental test of heartbeat pace.
Fashionistas steal the thunder,
Last year's gear's a great disgrace.
Each year I am stunned with wonder;
Hugging Lycra fills this place.

Fashionistas steal the thunder,
Last year's gear's a great disgrace.
Sighs, at my age, are a blunder
Though the thighs – and bums – are ace.
Each year I am stunned with wonder;
Hugging Lycra fills this place.

Sighs, at my age, are a blunder
Though the thighs – and bums – are ace.
My weak heart is torn asunder
With lust-filled thoughts that beat apace.
Each year I am stunned with wonder;
Hugging Lycra fills this place

The Diners

They sat in the restaurant,
facing each other;
a pale, indistinct woman
applying lipstick to her dreams,
and a grey-haired man in glasses,
his elbows supporting an iPhone
held delicately between bony fingers.
He was as absorbed in his precise manipulation
as he might have been
if the phone had been his lover.
Her absent look and his two empty glasses
defined the scale of their distance apart.

The Madrileña

She was an eagle, this Spanish woman,
this Madrileña, poised in the Metro.
Such a strong, angular face, fine features,
eyebrows an arched defence against weakness;

a proud woman, painted with bold brushstrokes.
Her eyes spoke unutterable sadness
as her hand brushed over the silver cross;
a silent prayer suspended at her breast.

Then she rearranged her legs just slightly
and, with this small gesture, she advertised
black silk stockings and exquisite shoes;
her triumph of hope over tragedy.

The Artist

He paints the spaces between his images
with as much care
as a poet writing behind the lines.

His puppet, a Pierrot figure,
lies slumped
on a narrow pavement,

with loosened strings,
no longer dancing
to the tune of war.

Each brush stroke licks around
memories of leaden soldiers,
as if they were ice cream melting

on a hot summer's day;
a foretaste of death
dripping on the nursery floor.

The Cuckoos

A pantoum sonnet

Cuckoo, cuckoo, a crazy cry again,
invasive birds would smash our Western yolks;
a mirthless sound that borders on insane,
that is the sharpened point of cartoon jokes.

Invasive birds would smash our Western yolks
with empty shells of reason gone astray
(That is the sharpened point of cartoon jokes).
Far right wing mobs on Paris streets today

with empty shells of reason gone astray
would kill jihadists, guillotining law.
Far right wing mobs on Paris streets today
would answer eye for eye, inflaming war.

Cuckoo, cuckoo, a crazy cry again,
a mirthless sound that borders on insane.

Unwritten Poetry

Each face a muted blank of engine drone,
No hint in aircraft aisles of human glee,
What lies within I fear I cannot own;
It's hard to read unwritten poetry.

In life we sometimes seem inanimate,
Ignoring neighbours till it is too late,
How much we miss when insular we fly;
Adventure lies within each mind nearby.

The Road to Salamanca

We drove to Salamanca, you and I,
a bleak greyness of snow on distant mountains,
the foreground rocky, harsh and unforgiving,
a landscape of grey-green ghosts and pining.

A solitary bull breathed thin vapour
across our final olive grove,
and fog swirled, licking at the edges
of our relationship.

The ancient town
disgorged
a soup of salt cod, spinach and chick peas
the last vestige of warmth
as daylight drained from the cobbled streets
and left us to face our reality.

The Depths

A *nove otto*

Such darkness swirls in pools of light,
The sky, the stars, the infinite,
Reflect the surface of the deep

Where fishes drown in amber dreams,
Where drowning is not all it seems,
For it implodes erotic sleep.

Transcendent tears, crushed pearls of salt,
Rip tides of love, a summer fault,
All break the surface, make us weep.

The Traveller

On his journey through life, he wore a coat.
In one pocket he put the places he'd been
Together with the notes for his poems,
And in another, the boarding pass and passport
To places yet to come.

As he neared his destination
He started to write poems
With a greater sense of urgency.

The poet can be in such a rush
When immortality calls,
Fearful that his final collection may be called
The Unfinished Works of…

Talking Turkey

I have a tale of what befell
At Christmas time, in Portugal.
We enquired in Portuguese
Of turkeys and of Christmas trees,
Then ordered both with greatest ease.

Though short-lived was our elation,
Something died in the translation.
The tree was good, there's no denying,
The turkey, though, was death-defying,
A two-man lift, and I'm not lying.

But we alas were only four,
And one was not a carnivore.
The oven was an ancient one
Devouring firewood by the ton.
This really made the cooking fun,

As at its best it just displayed
Boiling point in centigrade.
For fourteen hours we kept it fed.
The smoke filled room turned eyes to red,
Then at last we went to bed.

When we arose on Christmas morn
Full of cheer but rather worn,
There huge upon the table lay
A mighty bird, a fine display
Of cooking skills beyond gourmet.

I write this poem three days on
Nearly half of one side's gone.
Would that a book beneath the tree
Had left another recipe
For turkey pie just made for three.

In future when we're talking turkey
With grasp of language rather murky,
We will find out first of all
The local lingo word for small
Before we telephone our call.

The Scream

A rondeau

This child's shrill scream, a sawmill screech,
Held pain beyond the normal reach,
And filled my eyes with sawdust tears.
It cut the benchmark of my fears.

With wooden words I now beseech
The gods of whom religions preach.
Will Christ the carpenter impeach
The evil man who heartless hears
This child's shrill scream?

Thus growing trees are felled, and each
Will make a wooden box of beech,
And, with thin sticks of wrath, some chairs
To rock old age with night's dread mares,
For acid memory will leach
This child's shrill scream.

The Lesson

The small boy ran with a gurgle of joy;
The rest of us sat as the aircraft flew.
He raced up the aisle then careered anew;
Each journey adventure for this small boy.

Seems we were content, on our journey bent,
To be borne sedate from cradle to grave.
His joyful excursions skipped on the stave,
Butterfly movements, but we were content.

Innately we know that life is for play;
Meanderings give the greatest delight.
They do not alter the length of the flight
But they make each day a little less grey.

Pablito in Madrid

Pablito's of the Schnauzer sort,
He's debonair, though still quite short.
His barber keeps his beard in trim,
His coats are cut to flatter him.

He owns the streets of old Madrid
And swaggers like a new El Cid.
The baker bakes him special bread,
He wins all hearts, he's way ahead.

He has few faults but here are two,
It's never clear who's walking who.
His aim at lampposts ain't so sharp,
Those passing by may need a tarp.

He tangles leads with all the best
Where sniffing butt's the acid test
Of pedigree, of friend or foe,
Of mateship, or a bright new beau.

When Dave and Anna socialise,
It's with his friends contrariwise.
Without him they'd know very few.
He's the one with the howdy-do.

They take him to the doggy park
And let him loose to make his mark.
It is a place to let off steam,
To mix and mingle with the cream.

He races with the greyhound set.
If at the track, I'd place a bet
That he, the hare, would win the race
For there's no doubt he sets the pace.

The Invitation

A triolet

Let us go now to a foreign land,
That we may explore where hearts unite.
Though the shores may be made of shifting sand,
Let us go now to a foreign land.
There may we find, hand clasped in hand,
That the crest of a hill wafts love into flight.
Let us go now to a foreign land,
That we may explore where hearts unite.

The Sceptic

My God dwells not in churches
but in the hearts and minds
of those brave enough to build them.
He is made manifest by the Word
but is beyond the Word
in all its multiplicity of meaning,
and He is not constrained by it.

He exists in all creation,
even in me,
but there He is not alone.
His alter-ego, the Devil, is in me too.
My free will is the balance between them.
Must I upset this balanced
duplicity between good and evil
in my ignorance
as a thinking man?

Perhaps it is better not to eat of the fruit,
but instead to sit under the Bodhi tree and consider
the gravity of the situation,
until a rotten apple falls
planting seeds of godliness within.
In time I too shall become celestial compost
assisting re-incarnation.

That is my hope.
In the meantime, I have love;
stronger than faith,
more enduring
than knowledge.

The Cuckold

A rondeau

Oh, ring the bell! I'm wed to Sue,
the girl to whom I shall be true
until Jack Frost rules over hell.
This I swore, she swore as well.
Then o'er our nest a cuckoo flew,

and careless cuckold seeds did strew.
From those white seeds a dark egg grew.
Upon revenge my heart did dwell.
Oh, ring the bell.

From Hades frosts a cold wind blew
my oath towards the graveyard yew.
Her waist, my anger, both did swell.
Sue was fallen. My thoughts were fell.
Out, leprous spot! My love I slew.
Oh, ring the bell.

Spenser's Sonnets Unspencered

Though Spenser lays the senior poet's claim,
As sonneteer with interlocking rhyme,
Upon the scene that upstart Shakespeare came,
And simplified the sonnet for all time.

No doubt the older man eschewed the crime,
Unlacing his three stanzas from their stays,
But Willy did not give a silver dime
For fuddy-duddy Spenser's strictured ways.

And thus, since Socrates in ancient days,
Young men have undermined establishment.
Their elders think it just a passing phase
Until they realise its true extent.

Come, Edmund Spenser, leave the sonnet scene!
I far prefer your famous Faerie Queen.

Dolphins

I am filled with darkness,
the blinding dark of thought
that illuminates nothing
as I walk in the shadows,
looking in, instead of looking out,
for I am drawn to the depths of my being
and like to drown in them,

dragged into crystal caves
where Neptune reigns
in a futile pool of tears,
yearning for Salacia.
It is a choice…
We could just as easily disport with dolphins.

The Widow

Some years had passed,
And on a sudden impulse
I visited his widow.

I found her still life
A neat garden of memories,
From which she had excised
All weeds but sadness.

She grew sweet peas, and placed them on a window shelf
To mask the musty smells of the past.
Lace curtains filtered the sunlight
So that her photographs would not fade.
I saw, too, that the clock on her mantelpiece had stopped
At half past nineteen seventy-two.

She prattled on about her grandchild,
The phoenix of new love, risen
From the ashes of her past;
An insecure foundation, I thought.

My memories were
From the days of our youth.
They had been times of laughter.
I could not now inhabit her grief,
For it seemed to me a cancer,
More malignant than his.

I was relieved eventually
To escape her time warp of remorse
And to walk back into the sunlight again.

Next year we shall exchange Christmas cards as usual,
And speak, from a distance, of the good old days.

Fleas

A sestina

Let the sestina begin;
A French form of some complexity
That puzzles the mind of the poet
And causes some scratching out with his pen,
As if his poem has fleas.
Really, the end words do leap about so.

He is undaunted, so
Let him begin.
(Blast those flaming fleas!)
He thinks he can deal with the complexity
By shepherding the words like sheep in a pen.
A good sheepdog would be of great help to the poet.

I am the poet
And I am in control of this poem, so
Let my pen
Begin
To defeat the complexity
By splattering ink over the fleas.

Bother! Now the angry ink-soaked fleas
Attack the poet
Adding to the complexity
By biting him on the buttocks, so
He scratches furiously before deciding to begin
Again with the pen.

He now realises that the sheep in the pen
Have fleas.
After his fourth gin he decides to begin
Again, and again, and again, being a resolute poet
But now slightly sozzled, so
This adds to the complexity.

Shit! He can no longer pronounce 'complexity'
Instead he has a stab at it with his pen
But misses and pours himself another gin so
That he no longer feels the flaming fleas
And, being a perfectly pissed poet,
He now lets a lurid avalanche of alliteration begin.

The sestina is a real so-and-so because of its complexity.
My advice is to begin by not writing in pen.
Beware! The irritation of the fleas confounds the poet.

Written in Cobwebs

Caught in the nascent light of dawn,
a lifetime
written in cobwebs
on a dusty pane of glass.

The memories
flood back
as the sun's rays
surprise my face,
half blinding me
with overflowing warmth
and joy;

a warmth that soothes
the cavitation of a heart
caged in time,
like a fluttering bird,
its song remembered well,
if now but faintly heard.

Tendrils stretch
to gain the portico,
hoping it will hold aloft
the thin veins of truth
etched on leaves,
whose shimmering is backlit
by the sun god's promises.

So, too, the small red flowers
in their glass, Venetian blue,
desiccated now, and dead,
their petals fallen,
but their scent still held in memory.

Memories are strewn so carelessly,
across the table,
their reflection caught
by sunshine on the patina
of age.

At length, the sun goes in
behind a cloud;
it's time to break my fast,
for life bereft of dreams
lies in this new day
and beckons me.

Huge the Hurt

Alliterative verse

Monstrous murderers, on mayhem bent.
Huge the hurt. Their horror spreads
In wild wastes, woe-betiding,
With callous cruelty decapitating strangers,
Inhaling hate. Inhuman blades
Are bathed in blood with blessings cursed.
Gruesome rise the ghosts as the god-mistaken
Avenge like angels ascended from the pit.
Righteous religion the reason given.
No law of love, no lingua franca,
A blinded brotherhood imbued with hate.
We pray for peace. Peace is not their aim.
Yet we yearn. Universal is our sorrow.

Time Travel

A sonnet

In mid-Pacific on my flight back home,
the twenty-fifth of June, or so I thought,
I chanced to check it on my new iPhone,
a bargain from Hong Kong and cheaply bought.

It took me by surprise to say the least
to find it said I'd travelled back in time
into the twenty-fourth. I shook the beast
and cursed the vendor. What a filthy swine!

Just then the captain came along the aisle.
'Hi Jack,' I said. 'We need to turn around.'
He paled at that and quickly lost his smile.
Before I knew it, I was tightly bound.

My ignorance I rue within my cell.
The iPhone's fine. It was the IDL.

The Clock

Slow and stately ticks the clock
seconds breaking stillness
with pendulous monotony

to and fro
they go

into a haze of bygone days
and dust
suspended in the moonlight.

The lunar tick of the clock
drips time, drop by drop
Ere the cuckoo calls

to cut the thread
that binds us
to the metronomic madness
of the clock.

Ego

The Great I:
an erect symbol
of pens
and guns
and penile servitude.

www.ingramcontent.com/pod-product-compliance
Lightning Source LLC
Chambersburg PA
CBHW070929080526
44589CB00013B/1452